Cape Sounds

CAPE SOUNDS

Gavin Joachims Publishing
Shop 1A, 25 Voortrekker Road,
Goodwood
7460
gavinjoachimspublishing@gmail.com
Telephone: +27 (0) 21 591 3485

First published 2019

ISBN: 978-0-620-84312-6

Print and bound: Tandym Print

Cover image: Cody Losper

Cover design: Gavin Joachims Publishing (Pty) Ltd.

Psalm 127 King James Version (KJV)

1 Except the Lord build the house, they labour
in vain that build it: except the Lord keep the
city, the watchman waketh but in vain.

2 It is vain for you to rise up early, to sit up
late, to eat the bread of sorrows: for so he
giveth his beloved sleep.

3 Lo, children are a heritage of the Lord: and
the fruit of the womb is his reward.

4 As arrows are in the hand of a mighty man;
so are children of the youth.

5 Happy is the man that hath his quiver full of
them: they shall not be ashamed, but they
shall speak with the enemies in the gate.

Table of Contents

Thanking the sounds from home (by Taryn Haynes-Smart)

I wrestled with the question of what it is that makes the Cape sound truly unique. My logic discounted every sound I considered in my day: the traffic, kids on the school ground, even the birdsong early in the morning. These sounds I could hear anywhere in the world.

An early morning flight to Johannesburg reminded my heart.

Early morning flights mean leaving for the airport while my family and the neighbourhood are still sound asleep. I am awake before the birds. Their song fails to greet me when I open the door. In my house, the people (and one of the dogs) sleep undisturbed by my 3am alarm. The two cats can't believe their luck – me getting up at silly o'clock means adventure awaits them. They pace the floor and paw at the door in anticipation, bounding out into the darkness as the door opens. The ever-faithful Labrador would never dream of letting me wander around the house alone, so he stays close.

The early morning flight meant my "Good morning Mommy" greeting would have to wait until the plane landed, so I could play back the voice note waiting for me when I reconnected. Away from home, I would miss the next instalment of my daughter's imaginative forest tale, unfolding along the suburb paths as we walk to school. Urban transforms to lush forest floor with bears and foxes and other such creatures as she narrates. The sounds of chattering children signal our arrival at the school gates.
These sounds, so easily taken for granted, pierced in their absence on that quiet, cold, dark Autumn morning.

The Cape fills my day with diverse sounds from morning to night, some pleasing to my ears (and heart) and some not so much. I am not always conscious of them but take me away from this vibrant city just one night and I miss the sounds from my home. I miss the birdsong at home. I miss the sounds of the neighbourhood waking up, even the car alarm that routinely activates a few houses down. I miss the patter of my daughter's feet scampering down the passage and clambering into our warm bed for a morning cuddle before we get our day started.

As I drive to the airport, my head is focused on the roads I share with a handful of other early morning travellers. Yet my heart knows home, even amidst its many travels. It is standing with feet in the ice-cold Atlantic Ocean, listening to the seagull cries and waves lapping at the shore. I hear my daughter's squeals of intense delight as she plays with her dad in the breaking water.

Far from my home, the sound of grinding and heating and steaming mingle with delectable aromas of roasted coffee beans. As I wait for my latte, I am reminded of my Saturday morning local. I have landed in Johannesburg. I am thanking the sounds from home.

***

Without her knowing, Taryn Haynes-Smart was the push behind this book. I thank God for using you, Taryn. A loving Father we serve. Thank you, Taryn. God Bless you. Amen.

Awê Masekind (deur Samuel Theron)

Emo se awê masekind
ek beskou hom as 'n vrind.
Want ek ken hom as die bure se kind
wanneer hy praat, klink hy soos die Kaapse wind.

"Awê masekind" is die taal van die Kaap.
Ek skrik wakker uit 'n diepe slaap.
Staan op en ek hoor masekind
toe is dit my neef se kind.

Die skollie sê: "Awê masekind ko hier."
Nou weet ek hy soek iets; vir 'n skyf of 'n bier.
Heeldag staan hy op die hoek
met beide hande in die diep sakke van sy broek.

My neef se seun en ek raak aan die gesels.
Hy sê hyt nou diep lus vir 'n Bells.
Ons beide se kop is verskriklik seer!
Ek sê hom dis wat ons nou makeer.

Uit die verte hoor ek: "Awê masekind."
Herken die stem, dis 'n ou skoolvrind.
Hy vra: "Wat maak jy?"
Ek sê ek moet loop om die skollies te vermy.

By die huis geniet ons eers lekker dik sop.

Later gooi ek vir ons beide 'n stywe dop.
Sit gou die radio aan dat die musiek kan klop.
Neef se kind huiswaarts moet ek musiek stop.

Awê masekind, kan jy nie praat nie?
Alweer besig op die muur met grafitti!
Awê masekind doen jou ding.
Ek wil so graag sien jou tekening.

***

[Dis die lig, dis die blou, dis die broeklex wat ek kou, dis die gejaag van my mag, dis al.]

[Ek sê dinges hoe lyk dit. Ek en djy nykit. Lekker snug in my rubber duck...I think I might have added the last part along the way.]

[Djy maak jou froelaatie dik an.]

[Stiek yt jou bang ding!]

[Ken djy my ma?!]

[Witmense se goed...]

[What kine?]

[Hello! Hello! Waa wil djy wies?]

Akkeltjies (by Marius Williams)

The sound of the early 70s and 80s will stay with me till the end of time. The sound of Cape Music: Jonathan Butler, Lionel Petersen, Richard John Smith, Walter Brown and Zane Adams - The Rockets and Pacific Express. We danced till the early morning hours, in Cape clubs as far as Samburgh Inn (in Pniel).

On the platteland where I spent my early childhood, life was quieter. The people on the farms in the Boland were soft spoken. As a child, I had the impression that they lacked confidence.

In 1969, our family moved to Kraaifontein. My sounds changed. My hearing changed. For me, it was a drastic change. I was suddenly among the sounds in the Mother City. Here the natives and the foreigners tried to communicate. They developed sounds and a new language. So too began my new way of hearing. On my soft ears, the new sounds were almost aggressive: Loud! More people, more interaction and consequently more sounds, I suppose. Then, I perceived this as greater confidence.

In the early seventies I experienced more of the texture of the sounds of the Cape. The sound of street hawkers. Locations, like Arno in Scottsville and the corner shops in AME dorp, come to mind. Hawkers strung any combination of words to entertain and to sell. These sayings were almost hypnotic, inviting one to buy their goods: "Ek sê los dâi ou se goed, myne is stroopsoet," or "Is ja, ons wiet die sanksies druk, ma hie is jou geluk."

Every day after school, and when homework done, the sounds of kids playing kennetjie, hokkie, klipgatjie, pophuisie, wegkruipertjie, allies and kapping tol, filled the Lane in AME dorp. Sounds of playing are only interrupted when the familiar sound of mothers screaming and shouting, for children to come home.

On weekends, another sound popped up: During the day, young people roaming the streets with big double tape deck sound systems. Break dancing on the street corners near cafés. PM9 and PM10 batteries were used to prolong the life of the portable sound systems.

I was very lucky to also experience the sound of resistance. The sound of kids in the streets throwing stones from 1976 to the late 1980s. My best and ultimate sound was in 1983. Rocklands Civic Centre. The launch of the UDF. A mix of anger and jubilation.

People sound different in the various parts of our country. I am not merely talking about dialect and accent. I am talking about the akkeltjies: the animation that accompanies the sounds. Sometimes people say a little, but it sounds like a lot. How is that possible? With the following words: Isit? Is djy visieke? Duidelik. Gevalik. Jo. Né. Lekker djy. Nou soe nou. Nou wiet djy nou hoe? Awê. A lot is not only said, but given the context, even what is said is different.

These are my experiences of sound. Going back as far as 50 years. I have seen, heard, tasted, smelled and touched this sound. Most of all I lived this sound. My Cape Sound.

Sounds of prayer! (by Gavin Joachims)

On his way to destruction. My prayers not answered. I think I have asked in vain. I pray my faith remain. I continue to seek His Favour. Yes, even in my darkest hour His Love for me unchanged. Thank You Lord for Loving us. Thank You, Father, for your Grace on our lives. Thank You for Loving us first. May we appreciate Your Beauty, for this Earth continues to show us beauty, even in the midst, of evil.

I pray Dear Lord, that You cover us with the Blood that was shed for us. I ask this Lord for all of us, in Jesus Name. Amen.

We are all sinners. Judgment is His, only.

Crash! The sound that changed my life. Part one (by Kurt Abrahams)

In the early morning hours of 16 December 2009, my life and that of my family's changed dramatically. I was on my way home from a night out with friends. My wife received a phone call from the police informing her that I had been in a motorcycle accident. They told her that she should come directly to the hospital.

The first thought that entered my wife's mind was that my injuries were not serious. She says that she thought that I perhaps broke an arm or leg or some minor injuries. On her arrival at the hospital, she was informed by the trauma doctor that I sustained very serious injuries.

Meanwhile a huge group of bikers and friends gathered outside the hospital's parking lot, waiting on news from my wife. Doctors took between 3-6 hours just to resuscitate me. I was administered 19 pints of blood. Once they managed to stabilise me, I was transferred to the ICU where I was placed in isolation, attached to a respirator and numerous devices. The Head of Trauma informed my wife of my injuries and informed her that all they can do is wait and see as the next 72 hours were vital. The doctor told my family that I had broken practically every limb in my body. I sustained serious damaged to my skin covering my entire body, including head trauma. Doctors only discovered the following day that I had a burst artery in my right buttocks muscle which resulted in me getting septicemia. I developed kidney failure which required them to put me on a dialysis machine. Doctors had to perform CPR on me as I flatlined thrice. The third time my heart stopped beating for long and doctors were battling to get it beating again. Eventually the doctors were about to give up when the heart monitor started to indicate that my heart started to beat again. Little did I know that there was a power beyond that was going to change my whole life in such an immense way and give me a second chance in life.

While in ICU, in isolation, I was placed in an induced coma attached to all these monitors. Only immediate family were allowed into ICU. They could only see me through the glass doors and windows. Doctors could not perform any medical procedures on me due to the severity of my injuries. According to them, I looked like rag doll. For the next 6-7 weeks I remained in a medically induced coma. ICU staff could only do observations on me. I had so many people praying for me, people from different religions. I was told that people stood in small groups behind the glass confines where I was laying. They prayed for me. I got my second chance.

It happened on a Saturday evening, close to the end of January 2010. My eldest brother (Shawn), his wife (Wendy) and one of my good friends (Ian Farmer September) were gathered around me in ICU. They prayed for me. Suddenly out of know where, this very bright light shone in my face with intensity. I knew this was no ordinary light. I tried to cover my face and eyes with my hands, but I was unable to. I felt a weird sensation inside of me, which gave me a sense of total peace. Then I heard a voice say: “Don’t Be Afraid.” I could feel the presence of God right by me. That is where I accepted Christ as my personal saviour. Yes, I got saved.

The Sunday I noticed my eyes being placed on my legs and I could not move at all. I can remember saying that the helicopters were flying around in my room and that they here to fetch me. I was told that the drugs they administrated to me has this effect on people. Here I was thinking that I was losing my mind. My health was starting to improve, but doctors were still not allowed to take me to theatre and perform operations on me.

That Monday another decision was taken by the Head of Trauma. The ICU nurses had to cover me warmly with blankets, drips tucked under the blankets, and wheel me out of ICU; take the lift to the ground floor; and take me to the parking lot, where I could get fresh air and sunshine. After spending one hour in the parking lot I was taken back up to the ICU and attached to the monitors. This became a daily routine which I always looked forward to. In the beginning of February 2011, doctors were given the go ahead to perform medical procedures on me.

For the next two months, only plastic surgery and skin grafts were performed on me. I was wheeled into theatre twice a week for these procedures. Dead and damaged skin had to be removed almost entirely from the right-hand side of my back, including a muscle in my backside. Skin was taken off from under my right and left thighs and placed onto my back. The plastic surgeon also performed a procedure, called a flap, whereby he would build up my right buttock with skin taken from my upper right leg.
The recovery procedure was never easy for me. Just when I started feeling better, and when the pain subsided the next operation was scheduled. I was wheeled back into theatre.

I became a household name in the surgical theatres with the doctors, theatre staff and even the cleaners. One morning I noticed a new doctor standing at my bedside. He was going through my file. He introduced himself as the orthopedic surgeon. He was present the morning of my accident.

He lifted the blankets off me. He showed me a

long metal structure with pins protruding out of my left leg. It was an X-fixture which was keeping my bones together and allowing the bone to fuse. He further informed me about my other injuries. The look on my face turned from shock to horror...Tears. I could not believe what I was hearing. My body experienced immense trauma. The extent of injuries I had, is called polytrauma. It is commonly associated with injuries soldiers sustain in wars. My body was shredded.

After months in isolation in ICU and having had numerous skin grafts and plastic surgery, I was transferred to the surgical unit, where I was placed in a single ward for the control of infection. Every second day, two nurses would change the dressings on my wounds. This, another session of pain and agony. The orthopedic surgeon together with the plastic surgeon and the Head of Trauma, arranged a meeting with my wife and I, to discuss my injuries and how it will impact my life. They wanted to discuss the way forward.
We were told that due to my head injury and the severity of the breakages to my hips and other limbs, this resulted in calcification in my ankles, knees, hips and elbow joints. This is

known as Myositis Ossificans which left me unable to bend my arms, legs and ankles. The good news was that I did not suffer spinal injury. I still had all my feelings and sensations.

I had no appetite. My primary diet for the first four months after the crash was Freshubin [a nutritional shake] and morphine. Slowly my appetite returned, and I started eating very small quantities of solids. I preferred food from home. Everyday my wife brought me breakfast, lunch and supper. She had to feed me, because I was unable to flex my arms.
On many occasions I was unable to hold down the food. I had to spit some out. At times, I could not stomach the taste and the smell and the texture of food. The doctors discovered that the medication I was taking was causing my loss of appetite. They eventually prescribed other medication for me, which resulted in me being able to hold down my food.

After months in the surgical ward, I was transferred to the orthopedic ward to prepare me for my orthopedic surgery. Here the wards were modern compared to the other wards where I had been previously. The view from my bedside window was great. It felt as if I was staying in a penthouse. The following day I was wheeled into theatre where surgeons performed a procedure called manipulation. This is done under anesthesia. The surgeons bend the joints and work on soft tissue in order to improve the movement of the joints.

After waking up from the procedure, I experienced severe pain in all my joints. The slightest movement caused me to scream in agony. The pain was unbearable. The skin grafts on the bottom of both my thighs and back were still very raw and delicate causing severe pain as well.
Two weeks after the procedure it was decided that I would be admitted to a rehabilitation center to receive aggressive physiotherapy.

The day I was discharged from hospital, was a very emotional day for me. I was not just another patient to the staff. It felt as if I was leaving my home and family. Good friendships were created not only with the doctors, but with the rest of the hospital staff as well.

Ek hoor Mame se sê-goed (deur Mrs. Bosman-Adams)

My ma...jinne, nou wat ek groot is, dink ek terug aan die dae van my grootword. Ek het lekker gelag vir my ma se sê-goed. As kinders kon ons nie in grootmense se geselsskap sit nie, want dan word gesê: 'Tel jy tanne?' Of as jy op 'n stoel sit – wat vir die grootmense bedoel is – word jy gevra: 'Nou hoe groot is jou sterre? Want jy sit en meet dit mos nou!' Of wanneer jy geskel word en jy praat teen, word jy gesê: 'Maak jy van my bek 'n café!' En, moet nie probeer om jouself op te ruk nie, want dan word jy vertel jy is rammetjie-yt-nek.

In my tienerjare, en jongmeisie dae, het ek lekker gerinkenk. My ma het altyd gesê: 'Geniet jouself as jy nog jonk is, want as jy eendag kinders het, stop dit alles.' Ja, Vrydae was die lekker aandjie, en dan staan jy Saterdae op met 'n lekker babie. Maar, as ma in die kamer stap en jou wakker skree dan sê sy: 'Moenie nou kreen nie, gis'traand was jy mos katjie-van-die-baan.' Of as jy vra vir 'n pynpil word jy gesê: 'Gaan vra daar by dâi mense waar jy laas nag gekleter en geklier het.' En as die oggend na middag trek, en jy skarrel na die kombuis om vir ma te vra vir kos dan sê sy: 'Honger is dood van kruiwa stoot' of 'Aangename kennis honger, my naam is Susanna.'

Ek het nooit gevaag om my ma te 'jy' en 'jou' nie, want dan hoor jy: 'Kind praat jy met my soos 'n lap wat skeer?' Of as jy terug praat, dan word jy gesê: 'Ek sal vir jou klap dat die snot 'n kêtang om jou nek maak!' En moet tog nie sê dat jy moeg is nie, dan hoor jy: 'Dis van heelnag katterjak'.

Toe ek jonk was, het ons ouer mense gerespekteer.

"Ma, nou raak jy da'm oud. Kyk hoe vol plietse is jy."

Ek het altyd gewonder wat die betekenis was van 'bo blink, maar onder stink' tot my ma dit eendag gebruik het. Ek was besig om die skottelgoed te was. Dit was 'n halwe jop wat ek gedoen het. 'Nee,' sê my ma, 'Dis nou bo blink maar onder stink. Kyk hoe vuil is dit binne!'

So, ek probeer maar seker maak dat alles skoon is. Even as ek hoenderbene kou, maak ek seker daai been is nxare, soos my Mame sal sê.

Dankie ma (deur Jonathan van Beulen)

In stekende hitte was jy my koelteblaar.
In gierige weer het jy my, in bangheid kalmeer.
In dae van wanhoop het jy soos die hen
jou vlerke om my gevou...

So sal ek jou onthou, die sagmoedige ystervrou.
Bevoorregd was ek om 'n ouma soos jy te hê.
Iemand wat my altyd kon vermaan en verstaan.
Een wat bereid was om drome saam met my te
leef.

Jy het me geleer: Eers vergeet dan vergeef.
Respekteer en bly biddend voor die Heer.
In jou laaste uur, het ek gewens dat die tyd
nooit so aanbreek...

Wetend op aarde is ons maar geleen.
My laaste gesprek met jou, 'n ewige seën.
Flitse van my, suigeling. Tye toe jy in die koud
'n ekstra kombers om my kom vou...

My heg plek, jou rok se soom.
My inkruip agter jou rug.
Goeie maniere hoog op jou leer en jou tug.
Om God te volg jou plig. Ek mis jou koelteblaar.

Wie sal? (deur Gaireyah Fredericks)

Wat sal ek nou met my ure doen?
Wie sal ek bad en klontjies sjokolade een-vir-een voer?
Wie sal nou na my luister as ek die koerant hardop lees.
En wie sal my nou smeek om agter haar rug te kom lê en
saggies in haar oor fluister.

Nie sy nie.
Nie my ma nie.
Dis haar begrafnis.

Violence (by Billy Hendricks)

Mamma! Mamma!
I can't take it anymore.
The court is no more the same
I hate it!
I don't want to live here any longer
I'm afraid mamma
I'm afraid of dying.
Look at James
Look at John
Look at Shirley

They are all gone, they are dead mamma.
They will never come back.
Mamma, I'm afraid of dying.
Why must we live behind prison bars
in our courts, mamma?
"I can't take this place anymore"
"I can't stand this pain any longer"
It makes me sick.
All the time people are dying
All the time 'they' make peace and suddenly
the gang war starts over, and over again.
Mamma! Mamma!
The gang war is now on innocent toddlers.
It is just getting worse and worse.
"I'm leaving, I'm leaving tomorrow, this place
has no future for me"
I just hope Mamma, that you will understand...

Cape Noise (by Ané Williams)

Growing up next to one of the biggest shebeens in Cape Town, all I heard was NOISE.

As a child I quite enjoyed listening and dancing to the music during the day, but at night I was tossing and turning...struggling to fall off to sleep. The music was not the only noise that kept me awake. There were underlying sounds:

that of people chatting and catching up over bottles and bottles of beer; beer bottles falling; and glasses breaking when people had way too much to drink. Then arguments ensued, about who paid for the previous round and whose turn it was next. More than often, women arrived next door in their pajamas, dragging their husbands home, whilst hungry children are at home waiting to be fed. This was probably one of the saddest sounds in the community where I grew up: crying children.

Most men got paid on a Friday. Instead of taking their money home or buying food for their families, the shebeen was their first stop. There, some of them stayed most of the weekend with pop-ins at home. Although I was only 10 years old, I knew something was not right. Why would a father - knowing what the situation was like at home - ignore the cries of his children and loved ones?
Later in life, I learned about "die dopstelsel". This argument is by no means an excuse, but I believe that coloured people have been trapped in a cycle of alcoholism that have some of its origins in this vile practice where people of colour – mainly male farmworkers – who received their wages in the form of alcohol. Some took it to reward the week's hard work, whilst others drank to quiet the noise that was

waiting at home. Part of our history saddens me and the fact that we very willingly refuse to write our stories, leaves me heartbroken.

Yet, with all the hurt and all the pain - I know as a coloured community – church will be packed on Sunday mornings. Sundays at church was a "juig" and 'n "roering", with shouts of praise to God.

We later moved to Goodwood, and I found myself in a former white community. Things were different, yet I was always reminded of home, like when my best friend visited. We were both still in high school. One day she stayed a bit later than usual and had to take a minibus taxi home. I lived off Voortrekker Road; a very noisy road in Cape Town. The two of us were terrified. I gave her a hug as she jumped on the taxi that went to Bellville taxi rank. She then had to take another taxi to Belhar, where she lived.

I was back at home saying 50 Hail Mary's. I prayed for her safe journey home. When she got home, she phoned me and told me about her journey. By the time she got to Bellville taxi rank it was already dark, but the streetlights were on, the rank was still packed with people, taxis were playing loud music, and there was lots of laughter and cheers. The place was alive with sounds: People trading and a guy with no front teeth who walked up to her saying, “suckers R1”. Whenever I think of this story it makes me chuckle and say, *my Cape Sounds.*

Yet amid silent fears there is the quietness that our beautiful City gives.
Sunday mornings walking up Lion's Head, reaching the top, taking in the spectacular view and enjoying the stillness. Or, whenever my heart is troubled, I can go to one of our beautiful beaches, and stare in awe at God’s creation, God’s Greatness and God’s Faithfulness. In the stillness I hand over my troubles, make my decisions and from there I make my next move. My next sound...

The Cape sounds JAZZ! (by Gavin Joachims)

Beautiful to listen...
the many voices and
sounds on the streets of Cape Town.
Truly, the still of the mountain was given. Enjoy.
That still of God’s creation.
Majestic mountain motionless.
Steadfast like our God.
And, the sounds on our streets:

I pray that you forgive our sins Dear Lord.
I ask this in Jesus Name. Amen.

I pray that our communities again
echo with love and laughter.
Unafraid of the moment.
Free of fear, walking late at night holding hands.
Children playing in our parks.
Death:
Killings and murders...too common!
They have scarred us Dear Lord.
Lies invisible. This space that I was born in. Sin?
I pray, your Blood Lord Jesus, over all our communities.
Restore peace dear Lord Jesus, according to your loving kindness.
I pray this in Your Holy Name. Amen.

And Lord, may the Holy Spirit administer to our hearts, so that our bones may rejoice!

Crash! The sound that changed my life. Part two (by Kurt Abrahams)

Arriving at the rehabilitation center - UCT

Private Academic Hospital - a felt nervous and anxious. I had no clue of what was instore for me. I was wheeled directly into a single ward where I was transferred onto a bed with all my personal belongings on the bed as well. After a long while a nurse eventually popped in to take my details. I was then transferred to a general ward.

All the patients in the ward were disabled. I could see some had severe injuries and practically no mobility. As I laid in my bed looking at my surroundings, and the rest of the patients in the ward, the realisation finally kicked in that I was disabled.

The reception I received from the staff was not a friendly one. I was not sure whether they were too busy or whether this was their normal demeanour. I was immediately informed by the sister in charge that this is the rehabilitation section of the hospital and that physiotherapy is the key focus. I was further told that I was sent here for a specific reason and that it won't be an easy ride. I was told that it is hard work all the way. The following day I started to familiarise myself with the place, the people and the staff. It was very hard for me to settle in. It was a huge adjustment from Vincent Pallotti Hospital. It was a new adjustment and routine.

The head of the unit decided that I should be showered rather than have a bed wash. Her reasoning was that showering and the scrubbing of my wounds, would speed up the healing process. On the day of my shower, six nurses lifted me onto a steel stretcher. Pillows were placed under my wound areas and I was wheeled into the shower. Once placed in the shower, the nurse used a hand shower to wash me down. Excess blood ran off onto the stretcher, mixed with the water, as they scrubbed me down. Many times, I had bowel movements and urinated at the same time, as it was easier for me to do it this way and could be cleaned at the same time. It was not easy for me to do this in such a manner, but when you are in my condition, it is easier and better. The showering became a daily routine and it continued for approximately three weeks. Although it was not the most comfortable way of taking a shower, for me just being placed under the running water was better than being bathed in bed.

Later, a suction machine had to be attached to a wound on my right shin. It was back to bed wash. The machine would clear the wound from all the bacteria that was infecting the shin and prevent further infection. With each new day my wounds slowly started to heal except for a few that was in awkward places like beneath my thighs.

The next hurdle was not injuring the wounds while getting physiotherapy. Any wrong move would tear the skin beneath my thighs and the skin on my back. The physiotherapist put my feet into pillowcases to cover the wounds on my legs and feet. At this stage I could still only wear a hospital night gown because my wounds were still quite raw. I was given physiotherapy in my bed. My joints were still calcified preventing me from sitting up and standing on my own. The physiotherapist and occupational therapists could not do a lot with me because of my wounds and the limitation of my mobility however, this did not prevent me from going to the gym daily.
Although the exercises were done in bed, I was not given any leniency by the physio. My body

was pushed to the limit in my incapacity. As the saying goes "no pain no gain". In my case it was more like pain and more pain but somehow it made me not give up. I was still alive.

The gym was not huge, so it was quite awkward to be in it especially when one is wheeled in a bed into the gym and you had other patients receiving physiotherapy in their beds. The one thing that kept me motivated was seeing other patients that were totally incapacitated. Still, they managed to keep a smile on their faces. They kept me laughing with their sense of humor and their encouragements. Soon new friendships developed and grew between me and the fellow patients, with some of the staff, and with the patients' families and friends.

Ward 4F became my new home. It was the home for the rest of the guys and me. A wonderful bond formed between us, which helped each one us to cope and get through the day. There was constant laughter coming from our ward. The nurses named our ward, 'The comedy club'. Despite our physical conditions and mobility, we remained positive and always tried to cheer one another up when they were experiencing a bad day. Sometimes I would lay and just look at the patients trying to imagine how I would have coped if I had some of their injuries. Chatting to the other patients and hearing about their injuries and their personal circumstances, I had a deep sense of gratitude. God had given me a second chance in life. I had a family that He blessed me with. Things could have been so different if God didn't have His Hands of protection and healing over me, the morning of my accident. I started to testify to the patients, telling them how God had changed my life and what he has done for me. I started testifying to the staff and to whomever I met for the first time. With each new day I began to feel stronger physically, mentally and emotionally. Despite the painful wound care every second day and going to the gym with this broken body of mine. Eventually I managed to make a fist. I still could not flex my arms, but I began to get more functionality in my hands. Finally, I could grip and hold things again in my hands. It was such a positive boost for me.

After spending two months in the rehab, I was discharged and sent home to start a new journey of recovery and healing in all spheres of my life and that of my family's. It has been more than a year, since I had been home.

Saloet my bloedvoet (deur Mrs. Bosman-Adams)

Wat ek hou van die Kaap, is die taal. Dit is anders as wat ek praat in die Noordkaap. Byvoorbeeld die groet: Awê. En die ganster taal: Awê ma se kind. Waa haloep djy? Ma nee man!

Ek is gebore in die Noordkaap, maar is op 'n jong ouderdom Johannesburg toe met my familie. Toe ek 16 was, het ons weer terug Noordkaap toe getrek. Die praat in die Noordkaap was nou snaaks vir my. Ek het gelag toe ek die mense hoor praat by die huis. Dit was 'n aanpassing weereens van my moederkultuur. Dit was lekker luister en oornag, was my Noordkaap aksent terug.

Na my troue is ek en my man Kaap toe. Hy is van die Kaap. Ons eerste weke en maande in Atlantis was soos 'n deurmekaar in my kop. Ek kon die taal nie verstaan nie. Ek onthou hoe ek een keer vir my van gevra het: "Is dit wat hulle praat, Afrikaans?" Almal hier in die Kaap klink dieselfde. Kyk, in Johannesburg en die Noordkaap klink die wit Afrikaans verskillend van die kleurling en die swart Afrikaans. Maar, as jy met jou oe toe sit, hier in die Kaap, klink almal dieselfde.

Eendag, daar in Atlantis, sit ek een middag op ons stoep. Nie ver, in die straat, sit daar 'n paar jongens. My oë was op skrefies en my voorkop geplooi soos ek moes konsentreer om te verstaan wat hulle praat. Soos in kode het hulle gegroet en gelag en gevertel. "Het djy al tanne getrek?" het ek een hoor vra. En toe is dit 'hosh nkolosh' en 'pakamies' en 'wêk' en 'haloep' en 'nêma'... so luister ek na hulle vir 'n paar dae. Later daardie week, vertel ek my man van die kode taal. Hy lag en vertel my van sabela en vertel my hoe die manne praat en mekaar groot respek toon met die praat.

Ja die Kaap klink soos Emo en die klopse op Nuwe Jaar. Kleure.

My vriendin sy vir my een aand, "Kom ons gaan djol." Ek was onsteld. Ek het 'n man. Hoe kon sy dink dat ek op my man sal djol? Ek vind toe later uit dat die djol die disco club was. Lekker het ons gelag toe ek haar vertel.

Vandag is ek 'n Kapenaar. Ek is die taxi gaatjie. Ek is die gewemel. Ek is die karre wat drêg race. Ek is masekind. Ek klink en ek dink Kaap.

Saloet my bloedvoet.

Staying in Informal Settlement (by Samuel Theron)

Staying in informal settlement,
have little money to spend.
Brighten up the darkness at night
using candles as my light.

People dumping their waste material
for the children to play there, it's natural.
Scratching through waste for sellable things;
Exchange it for money to buy food and drinks.

Every morning I put on my overall and peak cap
pushing my trolley to look for scrap.
Walking the streets up and down
can't get home without the precious crown.

Now and then I cut the people's grass
to earn some decent money at last?!
With this money I can pay the kids school fees.
After paying the fees I will feel at ease.

My kids must get the best education,
so that they can stand tall in this nation.
They also participating in sport
Hoping, one day, they will be judges or prosecutors in court.

WENERA: The Story of a Wanderer (by Jurgen Namupira)

I watched the sun set slowly from the foot of the mountain. I knew of no place where I was to scrounge for my next meal. I could hear my stomach worms growl and scold each other, but I had no way to intervene. I wished I had a choice. Alas, the best I could do was lean on the cold brick wall and close my weary eyes. If death was to come, I'd rather have it find me dead asleep.

Eh! The days are short in winter this side of the world. Back home it never rained in winter. Here it rains cats and dogs...It is cold! I anticipated these situations to be normal overseas only. Here I was, soaking wet, shivering on an empty stomach just south of the Limpopo. Somehow, I missed home and thought of how I never slept on an empty stomach. Things sure changed.

Who ever imagined life can be such a miserable story to tell one day? We all ran away from a voodoo economy in pursuit of greener pastures. Little did we know that the grass is only green where there is someone taking care of it. I envied someone else's garden from afar and thought it was a lush field. I drew closer only to kiss my disappointment. Well, such is life!

Finally, I fell asleep; at least that was all I could remember before passing out. This was the beginning of a new story of a wanderer on a foreign path.

***

I woke up to a strange voice in my head,
Felt ecstatic –
my mind suspended in the unknown
no idea of who was talking to me.
He never gave me a chance to seek clarity,
hid his figure behind a glow
His voice with a wide echo.

I paid further attention and heard him call me to serve in the Lord's house. "It is time son," he said. Sounded like my late father; was it his spirit?

"Do ghosts really exist?" I thought to myself. Confused!

Back in the days I didn't even believe in this God. In fact, I didn't believe in anything... everything was mere coincidence and probability. I operated based on randomness, and so was my life. My father was a good preacher, he tried me and failed. I guess I was just in the process of meeting Christ and my time was not yet. I only saw the light beyond borders in deep sleep and on an empty stomach. One thing I always remembered was father's word about the 'damnation' of those who didn't want to receive Christ as their Lord. Alas, I was always adamant and never took heed.

I realised that this was a vision in my dream. It sounded like superstition, but it was what it was. He spoke to me in my sleep. It was his dying wish, the least I could do was maybe honour him. It was a hanging thought in my head. Sooner or later I would look for the so called, Yeshua.

I felt a sharp pain in my left rib and my heart felt like it was giving up. Still hungry, I shivered helplessly and struggled to open my eyes to look at the new sun. It wasn't the first time, but it felt different. They say nothing is new under the sun!

What sort of life was this? A university graduate with a first-class degree pass, at night out on vulnerable streets. When hard times came knocking on our doors, we tried so hard to manage the situation. Others were quick to throw in the towel and fled; we called them cowards. They went in all directions pursuing a better life. Some of them had a living God on their side to shine their paths. They found their breakthrough and their fortunes took an absolute turn. Their lives changed forever and for the best. They built new houses, new cars and married beautiful wives. They had the *dollars* to do all that without struggle. Me, I was still trying to find my breakthrough in the dilapidated streets of Harare.

I tried to hold on in the heat until my father breathed his last. Pressures of life began to mount, and without any support I could no longer stick around...hunting for small jobs, living from hand to mouth. I could not take it anymore and decided to follow others down South with hopes to put my degree to better use and have a job that paid. Only to realise, that not all that glitters is gold. In the streets of Mzansi I was robbed and left half dead the very same day I got off the bus. No-one to turn to. The friend who had promised to receive me, had gone AWOL.

I survived the days, but don't remember any that I enjoyed. I woke up to the cry of different victims, every day. The train was my alarm. What else could I do? I had no place to go until I decided to visit the church one day. I shared the story of my life and they welcomed my poor soul. I had a new family that spoke blessings to me and encouraged me to keep the faith and trust God's Will. The sound of His Voice, directing me to various places where I did find answers to life. Sounds of joy in the streets of Cape Town.

Tonight's the Night - It's the 15th (From '*Pleasures of the moment*' by Abednigo Mlesh Nyuka)

"Tomorrow is the 15th...I can't wait. For the past few days I have not had a decent sleep. Yes, I'm like a traveller, excited for a jolly good ride; a long journey. 12 o'clock mabhebeza, then sizokhiphamashankura. Afterwards we will party until the morning, just like we've never partied before...until the sun comes up. Plus ke, it's June 16 this weekend. It's Ayobaness. So, all I'm asking for is no wara–wara, no jealousy nhe babe wami - you're the only gal I care about

in this entire township. Here's something. Buy some etyme Joe."

***

"Yo tshoma, he gave me a thousand rand, sana. Plus, he bought us some electricity and you don't want to know how much," Noxy brags.

"How much?" they all ask inquisitively.

"Sshhh, please don't get excited it's still early days," and they all giggle. "As I said, my mother, my dad, and my brother – yes, even that scumbag got manna. The kids are so delighted. They got a R100 for school lunch for the month and R50 for sweets. My younger siblings are already sorted with their Christmas clothes. Can you believe it? No lay-buys, cash bantwana!"

"Still far from Christmas!" they all thrilled.

"Exactly," Noxy replies. "Still months left to go for Christmas carols," she laughs. "Now to cut the story short, tshoma, you know him mos. I mean, my brother that scumbag. Yoh, he's already calling my man, *Swaar.* That scumbag is such a parasite. Every five minutes 'Swaar this' and 'Swaar that.'"

Amajita can talk for hours, greeting each other like Americans. Noxy's job is to polish Thabo's army boots and his Tariyani shoes, scrub his takkies and jeans, and then she is guaranteed fun and access to all that is-good-is-nice.

"Sime, please run next door to Sis Pinkie's Spaza and buy a pack of powder soap so that I can quickly wash Thabo's combat gear," she instructs.

The gear was laying on the ground. His surname, Khumalo, written on the inside tags.

As soon as the soap arrives, the whole family is united as if they were slaughtering a cow. They washed the guest's *camouflage.* The next-door neighbours watched in amazement as the upstanding, yet often naively blinkered Noxy with her mini skirt and a white vest, shared loud enough for all to hear. She was voluptuous. Her water-dripping thighs and her pear ripe orange beaded nipples were eye catching to innocent strangers passing by.

"Hallo sisi?", "Hi there", "What's the hottest around the location", passers-by asked.

Yes, Noxy was the *Gossip Queen.* Those interested in what she was sharing came closer. Yes, Noxy had a *Blesser.*

"I have also been blessed with a chicken," she shares. "I must put hot water so that I can get rid of the white feathers, so that it won't fly away," she enthuses.

"Hold on tight," one close-by advises. "Good men are hard to find."

And, Thabo was a Blesser.

A man called, Daddy (by Dean Ramjoomia)

I have come to know the sound of his voice, loud and firm with soft hands, and a bearded face as he looks at me with smiling brown eyes. Daddy is his name, and he loves my mum. This I can see when he holds her hand.
But my daddy is all about hard work and little play.
He talks little about himself. This man who sacrificed his dreams and his friends to take care of us, his family.
Daddy is his name. I hear him often say: Do this, go there, or come here. Lots of rules and little time to play. That is the man I called daddy.
I have seldom seen him cry, but the frown on his forehead and the pain on his face tells me

that this man knows what it is like to carry a burden deep in his heart.
Despite the harsh words and commands, I have come to realise that this man, my daddy, cares about us.
I see him giving his last to us. He always buys us stuff.
Proud is this man in spite, of the little he has. His hope and dream that one day his children will have more than he.
Daddy is his name. Not much schooling did he have, but in how he provides and protects, I have come to know that my daddy is not just another ou.
Expressing love and affection, and the occasional laughter...this he does in his own peculiar way.
Few are his friends. In God is his trust. With strength he rises each day to face whatever may come in the day.

A father's heart?... (by Kudakwashe Munemo)

In the light of the day, I cast a tall shadow of an unmovable man of steel. I carry an image of a tough giant. My voice commands and booms like an army general in charge of some amateur recruits, but by night I cast a lone figure. I whail like a pierced buffalo. I have no heart of stone, I am vulnerable. I have the heart of a father who weeps for a son. Yes, I have the heart of a father.

Son listen to the confession of your lost father. I was young and foolish. I was a coward. No, I did not reject you...I was afraid. I turned my back on you when you were in your mother's womb. I wasn't ready to give up my nights out with buddies. I had no resources to take care of you. I couldn't risk my freedom, because I was still a child at heart. Today is not an easy walk to freedom. I am a prisoner on an island not inhabited or accessed by the living. I am serving a self-imposed life sentence. I think of you every night. I am not a child anymore. I have the heart of a father!

Rivers of tears flood my pillow. I was not there to feel your tiny feet kick your mother's tummy from inside her womb. I was not able to provide when your mummy craved for fruit at night. I was not in the ward when she writhed in pain; as she laboured in pain. I was not dead. I was partying with friends. I was not there to welcome you to this earth. I was not there to give you a name. I was not even aware that you existed. Today I have a heart of a father.

I shudder when I imagine you calling another man, 'dad'. This gets my blood boiling! I have no memories of your childhood. I have no visuals to enforce my imagination. But, deep down in my heart, I know I am your father. I see you approaching down the road. I run to hug you. It is only my imagination of you I have never met...all I know is that I am your father.

By divine order, I am your father. Through biology you carry my DNA. I won't give up on you. I can't turn back the hand of time. Wherever you are my child, I think of you every second. I pray for you. I plead guilty to my case. I have no moral ground to be called your father.

The Man by the Peppercorn Tree (by Gavin Joachims)

There lived a man by the Peppercorn Tree.
Upon a night he called on me.
So, I asked the Abbajah for his help.
This would my first, here, mission be.
This youngest child, just up from knee.
On a starlit night, in Autumn's height,

I met the Man by the Peppercorn Tree.

"Please, pray for me?" his first words said.
This dream, this form, this man long dead.
So, I asked the Abbajah for his help.
This youngest child, just up from knee,
put aside all reverie.
He spoke with the Man by the Peppercorn Tree.
"Is this the reason, why you were calling me?"

It's so he learned of this story told,
about this life that to death was sold.
So, I asked the Abbajah for his help.
I prayed for the Man by the Peppercorn Tree.
This youngest child, just up from knee,
had seen beyond what eyes could see.
On this starlit night, in Autumn's height.

His name was Links, this poor young man.
He came from some discarded clan.
And in those days, I shared his tears,
he asked that these here words do strive
to tell the story of his life.
That Man I met by the Peppercorn Tree.
This tale the Abbajah shared with me.

Outside the graveyard, all forlorn.
Lay the bones of a young, who 'fore dawn
had decided to end his own life.
I pray that Jesus Blood does free,
all the souls that in captivity be.
There lived a man by the Peppercorn Tree.

Upon a night he called on me.

***

Who was the man by the peppercorn tree?

Many years ago, I had a vision: A book called, Cape Sound.

When I was 3, my parents found me in our backyard in the middle of the night. It happened many times. They were at first alarmed, but later let me be. They could not understand how I unlocked and opened the stable doors of the kitchen, to go outside and be with the stars.

There was more that happened during those starlit nights. I met Links, there by the peppercorn tree. He told me many times the story of his life. As was a young child, I could hardly understand everything he shared, from where he grew up in some farm place, and of how this place by the peppercorn tree had become his prison. Links wanted to be free.

I don't know how Links died. I know that his soul was bitter. He asked forgiveness earnestly.

When I was 28, I was taken on a journey. At the time, I did not understand why I had to leave. I thought I was going away to die in a foreign place; on foreign soil. For five months, I hitchhiked through Southern Africa.

Before I left, the Lord spoke to me in the clearest voice. I asked Him to use me. I shared with Him the desires of my heart. He told 'Go my boy, Go.' A beautiful peace filled me.

I have learned how desires of the heart are made real. Today, I know that we ask God's blessing in all we do. Yes, desires of our hearts come true despite of us. Asking God's blessing in all we do; it is seeking first the Kingdom of God. Then all the things are added...even more than what we had asked for. Doubt makes our asking reserved, but our Lord gives abundantly and beyond our imaginings. Ask Him and give thanks even for the things unseen.

On my return to Cape Town, I had to go and meet with two people: One was my aunt and the other our neighbour where I spent the first 6 years of my life. My aunt was the easiest meeting. I phoned her and asked to meet with her. She did not ask any questions...almost as if she knew this day would come. Now, she was a reborn Christian. We sat and spoke in her kitchen. I told her that the Lord had asked me to meet with her and that I had to tell her that I forgive her, for the wrong against our family. She broke down in tears. She thanked me. She thanked God for sending me. We prayed together, and thanked God.

Later, I went to visit my neighbour where I grew up in 6th Avenue. I asked her about Links. She was shocked! Many unexplained things had been happening there. She was not willing to talk much about these things. She took my hands in hers, and with tears rolling down my face, she asked me to forget. I respected her refusal to share. She hugged me and I left. As I drove off, I was reminded of a promise I made when I was 3.

Some time back, I sketched a man resting against a peppercorn tree. At first, I did not know what it was: this man resting in the shade of the tree. As if in a dream, Links told me that it was he. I prayed for Links. I prayed for the forgiveness of his soul, for he asked me once more to do so.

"Dear Lord, in Jesus Name, I ask for forgiveness for Links. Forgive his soul, I ask in Jesus Name. Amen."

"Dear Lord, in Jesus Name, I too ask forgiveness for me: forgive my soul. I ask in

Jesus Name. Amen. And, I ask for Your Divine Blessing on this book Dear Lord. I ask this in Jesus Name. Amen."

I can't remember what I did with the sketch of Links. I knew that it had to be on the cover of one of my books: That sketch of Links.

I have now been told that it is okay that I lost that sketch. For, the picture had changed. The young man is laying under the peppercorn tree no more. His bones are rejoicing, and he is playing his saxophone Praising God our Father Almighty.

Bushy hair...don't care (by Ané Williams)

Since we were little girls, we were conditioned to think that beauty has only one face. Unfortunately, that meant blonde straight hair, blue eyes, fair skin and a slim nose. As a coloured girl I was aware that I fell short of description. I have bushy hair. It was a problem for everyone. My mom, sisters and even hair stylists complained about my hair.
Going to the hair salon was unpleasant. Once

a stylist mocked and said: “Hoooo, djy sal moet terugkom om jou hare te potjie.” I nodded, look up and smiled, but knowing that I did not want to relax my hair. Relaxer would affect the curl pattern of my hair and curly hair was my hairstyle. But my hair had to be relaxed, blow dried, pulled and tugged before I got any compliments.

Looking back, I realise that my hair wasn’t the problem. The problem was the need to conform. I did not embrace my natural self. In fact, everything makes sense now. I guess, life makes more sense when we allow things to be, just as God had intended, with free will to change the things that we cannot accept and the wisdom to discern.

My hair journey has been interesting. I am learning about my hair type, and the natural products that assist hair’s health. I am learning how to embrace and treat my hair. Yes, I get stares, remarks and questions about my hair. Today, in a beautiful way, I am loving my bushy head full of curls. I can jump into a pool whenever I feel like it. I can take a shower without a shower cap. And I can go to bed with a swirlkous. Going to the gym and going for a run is no longer a problem, it's my natural hair.

This hair doesn't care.

Kinderjare (deur Donovan Beukes)

Rooi gepantser in klokbroek en al
Die sewentigs is gevul met nuwe klanke
Sondag rituele sluit in kerk en koeksisters
Buite waai die wind sand aan
Radio blêr 'Ek verlang na jou'
Wie's dit ma? Sonja Harold is haar naam, kind.
My eerste Afrikaanse note uitbasuin
So raar en nie weer vir lank daarna
Die tafel gedek, dit dwing respek
Tafelberg staan en terg; gooi skaduwees
Wêrelde weg vanaf hier op die vlakte
Drome begin, tuimel, vat raak

Die trein huil, sny oor verdeelde spore
Die berg in sig, o hoe pragtig dis gewis!
Hoekom ry ons derde klas? My suster stel my gerus
Ek skud kop maar geen verstaning, andere loer my so

Ek voel skaam in die stad, my Kaap, hulle stad!
Die bergies stink hul vra om hulp en rinkink
Wie is daai? vra ek fraai. Ek word weggeruk en sluk...
Blonde koppies stap orent, ek glimlag maar hulle loer my so...

Die eetplek is vol, voel uitgesluit. Waar's ons mense dan?
Eetgerei word uiteengesit, neergegooi, kortaf gevra wat ons wil hê
Hoe ongemanierd! borrel ek; my suster ruk weer aan my
Andere loer my so, praat saggies onder mekaar

Ingelaat in hulle wêreld, moet nou weer terugkeer
Ek voel nog steeds snaaks, kan nie verstaan
Die trein kreun op verdeelde spore, draai weg...weg
Die berg blou, nou spikkelmooi, dan in rooi getooi soos die son sak

Veilig by die huis, die herinneringe bly; wat's verkeerd met my?
My vrae onbeantwoord, my tong gewikkel in kinderlike stryd
Die klanke voer my mee; 'Trein na Matjiesfontein', "Mamma dis Sonja!"

Ja my kind, kom help my gou...los nou die radio...
Buite waai die wind sand aan...

Crash! The sound that changed my life. Part three (by Kurt Abrahams)

Coming home after having been hospitalised for a year was an exciting moment for me, but also a very scary one. On the way home I recall the guys stopping at the motorbike shop where I used to hang out. I was not sure how I was going to handle it, when the others saw me. The expressions on their faces said a lot. Some were happy to see me, and others could not find words to say when they saw me laying on the mattress at the back of the van. I had a smile on my face and to break the ice, my first words were: "They don't call me Die Hard for nothing. I told you I will be back." Laughter erupted and they all commented that 'mal Kurt is terug'.

Pulling up in front of my house I was consumed with this overwhelming feeling of happiness, joy and anxiety. Many of my neighbours and those living in the street, walked over to the van to get a sneak peak of me. I felt like a celeb. But there were others who had tears in their eyes when they saw me.

It was extremely difficult to get me into the house. I had to be carried on the mattress. Those who carried me were extremely nervous and cautious. They carefully navigated the way through the house and into my bedroom, making sure they don't hurt me in the process. I finally was lifted onto the special hospital bed, which could accommodate me in my condition.

It felt strange laying alone in a separate bed at home. I felt strange not being able to lay next to my wife in our bed. My first night at home and the weeks that followed were not good at all. I cried myself to sleep.

Each new day was a battle. Besides the pain that my body still endured, I was in turmoil coming to terms with my disability and my situation. My communication with God started to fade. My faith and trust became weak. I made it very unpleasant for my wife and my two daughters to be around me, due of my negative mindset and attitude. The blame game started. I blamed everyone. I even questioned why God did this to me. I felt like a failure, a liability to my family. I felt like I was of no benefit to them.

I was no longer a productive person. I felt I was a burden, and soon I fell into a deep state of depression, the same that the psychologist warned about. Yet, I could not prevent it. I had suicidal thoughts, despite the antidepressants and other tablets to suppress the depression. Nothing seemed to work. I was at the bottom of a pit...total darkness with no escape. The longer I remained depressed, the deeper I was sinking into this dark hole. I cannot describe what it is to be in such a state of depression. What I now know, is that it is not a good state of mind. It is very difficult to rise from there.
Around the same time, my employer stopped giving me a salary as all my leave, sick leave and other benefits were depleted. I was declared medically unfit to work and was medically boarded. I refused to accept this because in my mind this was a temporary incapacity. I thought I would get better and would be able to resume my work duties again.

The impact on my finances, my home and family were enormous. I remained stubborn, thinking that I could change the situation. My family told me to accept and move on. But one cannot move forward, if you don't let go of the past, for then the past will always dictate your future. Forgiveness is also a very strong tool because by forgiving you heal quicker in all areas of your life.

I now found myself in the situation where I had no income. It seemed that the knocks were now coming from all directions. Things began to spiral out of control when my eldest daughter was laid off from her job. She was forced to give up her flat where she was renting and to move back home. The school which my youngest daughter attended sent me a letter informing us that they were suspending my daughter from classes if the arrear school fees were not settled very soon. The banks threatened to repossess my house and my vehicle. Soon I fell into arrears with my medical aid. This I could not afford because I needed to undergo more medical procedures. The medical scheme eventually suspended my membership and only agreed to reinstate once the arrears had been paid in full. This not only affected me but also my wife and youngest daughter as they were both dependents on my medical aid.
There were so many things happening to my family and I. The bond we had as a family was weakened. The situation at home was tense.

I turned once more to God. Amidst all that was happening to me, I had let Him out. I knew that prayer and allowing God back in my life would ease my burden and that I did not have to battle alone. I started to pray and called out to God to help me and my family. I asked Him to take us through the storms and battles we were facing. I continued to pray. I remained focused on His Word and His promise. The Word says faith as a small as a mustard seed can move mountains. Sometimes we forget to pray and thank God for His blessings that He bestows upon us even when we are going through difficult times. As I continued to pray and make God part of my daily life, I started to feel more at ease and my state of depression and anxiety started to fade slowly, day by day. My faith and my trust had been restored. An overwhelming sense of joy fill me. I was no longer afraid. My financial worries grew less, as I took each day as it came. God started to send people into my life and home from all over. Neighbours who merely greeted before, came to our assistance in various ways. Some provided us with groceries and other commodities; some helped us financially; my one opposite neighbour filled up my wife's car with petrol on a weekly basis and ensured that our kitchen cupboards remained filled with groceries and other necessities. We never went without basic services like water and electricity. The blessings kept on pouring in. One of the humblest acts was when the bike club I belonged to - Freedom Riders - held a fundraiser for me and my family. It was a huge success. When I was informed of the amount they managed to raise on the day, I burst into tears. Words could not express my gratitude for the generosity shown to my family and me. The money came in very handy. I paid up some bills and still managed to spoil my family a bit. Not only was God sustaining me and my family financially, He was also healing me physically, spiritually and emotionally. This never cost me a cent. Yes, God does answer prayers, we must trust and believe in Him. All in His time.

You People (by Marius Williams)

1994...the year of our Freedom. Our first democratic election. The sound of freedom. The sound of freedom in the workplace: BEE, Employment Equity, Labour Relations Act,

Basic Conditions of Employment Act, and no discrimination in the workplace.

I worked for the Post Office at the time. In the eighties, employees of the Department of Post and Telecommunications could only apply for positions in areas of their racial classification. A few token appointments were made before 1994. To test the waters, the top structures only approved positions of people of colour in the so-called white areas as assistant postmaster and superintendent. Not in charge, second in charge or just a supervisor.
We could now apply for postmaster positions in areas where we were not allowed to apply for before. We were skeptical, ambivalent. 'How would the people receive us in those areas? What would it sound like? What will the customers say when they see us?'

I was used to the sound of the customers in the areas that I worked, the so-called Coloured Areas. When the queues were long you would hear people say: "Julle base moet vir ons oek so baie klerke gie soes wat hulle het!"

In 1996, I applied for and was appointed as the postmaster in Gugulethu. I was received with open arms. The sound was amazing. My own colleagues and even superiors were negative and said that 'they' will steal my car and murder me in the township. In contrast, it was the sound of acceptance.

I learned Xhosa and started speaking to the customers in their mother tongue. The staff and customers were very impressed with me. I was an ambassador for the sound of the new South Africa.

In 1998 the sound quickly changed when I was appointed as postmaster at Howard Place Post Office, in Pinelands. The customers put me to the test to see if I knew my work.
When parcels were delayed, customers would utter things like: 'Since you people started working here our parcels started disappearing'. It is funny how a simple word like 'you' can sound in the context of 'you people'. When a white person says it, it's everyone except white.

In 2004 the postmaster concept was changed to branch managers. I was appointed as the branch manager of Claremont Post Office. I thought that the sound will change. It did not. In 2005 I applied for a transfer to Parow Post Office. It was closer to home. I was very excited as I thought that the Afrikaans speaking customers would be better than English speaking customers. I thought that the sound would change, but I was wrong. I heard words like: "Kry weer meer Wit tellers, julle diens is pateties."

In the last part of the 2010 decade a person could sense that people were more accommodating to what happened in the public sector. People complained less. The sound changed as people started to focus more on the general politics in the country, especially the President of the country, Jacob Zuma. The sound of the 2010 Soccer World Cup also contributed to calm the population.

Sound travels everywhere. Sound can change a nation.

Die bergie maak reg vir slaap (deur Samuel Theron)

Ek sien die bergie voor die viswinkel sit en gaap.
Hy lyk moeg! Maak hom reg om te gaan slaap.
Liggaam in klomp koerante toegedraai

beskerm hom teen die koue wind wat snerpend waai!

Hy lê en dink oor die dag,
maar wonder ook wat gaan gebeur deur die nag?
'n Bottel staan langs hom,
hy kyk daarna en sy verrimpelde gesig blom.

Bring dit nader en vat 'n stywe sluk.
Half pad deur lyk dit of hy verstik.
Hy het heelnag deur geslaap.
Hy hoor die taxi gaatjie skree: "Kaap!"

Douvoordag is hy op
maar voel hy het 'n dowwe seer kop.
Polisie besoek gereeld, maar is meer las!
Winkel trollie is die bergie se kas.

Met sy trollie op pad na sy volgende bestemming,
stop hy eers in 'n rustige omgewing.
Krap in die vullisdrom en kry 'n verslete kombers.
Voor hy weer gaan slaap, lees hy 'n bybelvers.

Home (by Billy Hendricks)

Come with me home
Come with me home, Cape Flats.
Come with me home fathers and mothers.
Come with me home children
Yes, come with me home.
The silence is broken.
Can't you feel the emotion?
We are caught up in violence.
Please! Come with me home
"let we take back our streets"
"let we take back our schools"
Come with me home, our communities.
Come with me home, Come with me home
There are hills and mountains between us
Drug lords!
Gangsters!
Corrupt policemen!
Corrupt politicians!
Corrupt lawyers!
I wish you are here, to come with me home
But you hold the keys
Yes, the key to violence.
Will you come with me home?

Ryk mister kaalgat (deur Dean Ramjoomia)

Daar loop hy, met sy kop inni lig en sy hande inni sak soos baas van
die grond waar op hy loop.

Kaalgat is die jong want geld het hy min maar klere aan sy gat laat hom lyk soos a lani vani Plain.

Sy hare is gekam met roller in sy sak want vir hom moet sy kroes hare plat lê op sy skewe kop.

Die ding like 'n lekker meit aan sy sy, cause vir hom sonder 'n girl is soos a moffie sonder a burg.

Daar loop hy met 'n bottle Klipdrif in sy hand want die ou het mos style maar geld virri brood het hy min cause hys mos die ou.

Snot neus is sy laaities, twie by die girl wat by Edgars wêk, en drie by 'n goose wat vir Bonwit wêk.

Ryk mister kaalgat is vol van style maar geld het hy min die kaalgat ding.

Maar brêkgat is hy, want by the way hys mosi

die ou van wie almal die stupid girls hou.

Wild Stallion (by Billy Hendricks)

I was once like a wild stallion
running wild up and down
In the plains!
In the fields!
Wildly free to come and go with a gangster mind
So cold yes ice-cold.
A wild stallion yoked to a chariot.
Yoked to a gangster chariot.

I was the devil's stallion.
I was wild yes very wild.
I was ruthless, fearless stallion
running wild up and down
In the plains!
Wildly free to come and go with a gangster mind
No one could ride me
No one could stay on my back

Until one day
He trapped me with a message.
They trapped me with a song, "Rock of ages"

It happened so fast yes just like that
He said to me, now you belong to Christ.
I yield, listen and obey.
And from that day, I was no wilder.
If you meet me one day and look at me,
You will never believe I was that wild stallion.
"Lion heart"

Free Spirit (by Jurgen Namupira)

She just wants to be alone,
lonely with her own thoughts...
embraced by nature,
wishing she could hug the wind;
whisper into her ears
'take me with you please'
truth be told,
she's sick and tired of being sick and tired,
she smiles
she laughs
she shouts
yet she sheds dry tears.
We see them not,
for they are hid behind the mountain of courage,
covered under the cloud of hope.
Here we are today,
praising the visible beauty,

when she's busy fixing the inner beauty, we broke...
the heart has bled,
and emotions have sped into her mind
knocked her down to her knees
but she's still fighting.
I hope we won't charge her for locking the world outside,
she needs to heal and pick us one by one
selecting only the worthy vine to produce tasty wine,
one day's one day
it shall be well for the free spirit,
and she shall sing of the good new days
emanating out of the brutal past.

Dearly Departed (by Gaireyah Fredericks)

Oops, another kick, so strong is he. He curls and turns as happy as me.
He yanks the cord and plays and bends, my fear confirmed, the term could end.
She seldom sleeps, a strong-willed soul. She shadows him and make HER known.
She kicks and turns but stays her side. Him on the right she plays with pride.

“Yes sister, no brother, has our time come? The walls are pushing, we’re not yet done.”
Obedient and content he crawls forth the light.
Stubborn and willful she refrains from sight.
“Nurse! Doctor! My son has arrived.” A cord so frail, delicate, but death denied.
“Good heavens Mum, it’s way too early.” Nurse, at this stage: “Do you think it’s worth it?”
A breathing soul, I think...I feel. “How can they question and not just heal?”
I beg. I plea for some attention. There’s one more child I need to mention.
Long talks, consults, deliberations. Frustration, pain, fear, no accommodation.

The ambulance turns swiftly, I roll to and fro.
Attendants keep hammering, “No birth Mum, breathe slow.”
Two patients to drop, before I am seen.
I feel her kick three times being moved in between.

“Farewell dear Mum, they won’t let me stay.
I yearned, all this time to meet you someday.
Well, never you mind, the time has come.
For my departure, take care of your son.”

“Nurse! Nurse! This machine is at fault!
Positioned correctly, but no heartbeat is called.
Dear God, my sweet princess, you lay paused
inside me.
With few tears I whisper: “Come forth let me
see.”
Bigger than brother, stronger in built.
Despondent, defeated, THE power has willed.
Cradled, hugged, a kiss on the lips. Clinched in
my arms, while I come to grips.

“Day two, dear son, hold on, I am coming.”
His lungs suffer greatly, yet he is still
summoning.
The ambulance turns swiftly, my princess is
closed.
My heart is still beating, but her heart is froze.

My son, pull through, I command you to fight!
Obedient, content, he struggles with might.
I’m selfish dear husband, permit me to say.
“Dear son I am proud but be on your way.”
Minutes or so that we last spoke. He acts up
and flat line, a sever final stroke.

“Dear Mum and Dad, we did what we could.
The machine wills his organs now, it’s out of

our hands.
We conclude our stay and sign the forms. While I walk the passage, I question my norms.
My son has left and so my daughter. My dreams depleted; my heart's been slaughtered.
It will pass, this pain inside. The loss, the emptiness, my kids had died.
So now when the absence is too strong to console,
I take a pen and ink my thoughts that wonders in my soul.

Eeue oue getuie (deur Donovan Beukes)

Eeue oud is jy O Tafelberg, stygend na die hemele
Net God verberg die waarheid, die stryd, ons stryd...
Omring deur fynbos en malende koue waters; gepunte rotswande
Op die wit sand dwaal groepies strandlopers in jou skadu
Hul eie taal, kultuur en struikelblokke; kyk hoe hardloop die bokke!

Jy verkyk jou aan die lewe daar onder en wonder gedwee

Is daar nog harmonie en liefde?
Of klief haat en nyd deur jou wolkekombers?
Eeue oue klanke weerklink na bo, die geruis van stemme moelik om te glo
Lewens aan die verander, gevoelens borrel oor, vreemdelinge sit voet aan wal
Seile bol in die stormsterkwind, jou prag gewaar, aangestaar,
trekpleister gewaar!

Dis 1647, die boot in gevaar, 'Niewe Haarlem' sy naam, Nederland se trots
Dit bots teen rots en brandergevaar; geen soeklig gewaar, gestrand, aan die brand!

Oorlewendes vertoef een jaar; roep om redding, geen boot in sig, fort gestig
Nie lank daarna; uitkoms op die horison, glimmende son bring uitkoms
Twaalf bote kom te redde, gelei deur W.G de Jong

Die jaar 1652, Van Riebeeck gestuur om te bestuur, ontmoet inheemse groepe
Jy verkyk jou aan die bollewange, seile wit gekalk, hoe fraai dink jy dalk!
In jou onkunde verwelkom jy hulle, nooit kon dink aan wat hul sou doen
Die eerste stukkies land van Khoikhoi aangekoop in 1671; nooit sou hulle versoen, die daad gedoen!

Die stam verloor hul hart, bring verdere smart,
kultuur besoedel, bande gesmee; o wee,
jou hart geruk,
jong Khoi meisies gepluk...

Khoi tolke dien as bemiddelaars,
onder andere, Herrij, Doman en Eva
Sy, as jong kind ingeneem in die Fort,
haar taalvaardigheid van groot nut
Ambassadeur vir haar mense dien sy as tolk.

Gissinge veroorsaak struwelinge
tussen nuwelinge en inheemse volk,
haar naam beswadder, emosies omhoog
Jy fluister deur die verraad,
wil nie luister, kweek verdere kwaad.

Franse Hugenote arriveer, jou hart word seer,
jou speelplek oorgeneem
Hulle is vlugtelinge, weggedryf uit vaderland,
nou onder nuwe beleid veg hul die stryd,
maar helaas, Nederlandse onderrig word verplig
Franse identiteit ontwrig, taal verdwyn, hul gees weggekwyn...
Die wynland hul voorland, hul nuwe land,
jy weer aan hulle kant.

Massas Khoi volk deur koloniste uitgewis,
jy verstar jou aan die geweld wat woed.
Aan jou voet, andere weggedryf noordwaarts,
daar gestop deur die San,

hul ander vyand; vee gesteel, onwettig gedeel,
ook hulle word platgevee…
Slawe ingevoer van verre lande;
Indië, Madagaskar en Mosambiek, ook die verre ooste

Kleurlingkind gebore vanuit gemengde oorde,
sy plek nie ten volle ingeneem…

Eeue oud is jy, O Tafelberg, stygend na die hemele
Net God verberg die waarheid, die stryd; ons stryd…

Ek sit by die see (deur Samuel Theron)

Ek sit by die see,
geniet die rustigheid terdee.
Ek hoor die branders se gedruis.
Hier voel ek sommer tuis.

Sien 'n hoë woeste brander
later na 'n kleine skuimende golfie verander.
Die see het altyd so 'n kalmerende effek
Beslis 'n positiewe uitwerking op my, direk!

Ek sien 'n man wat op die water roei.

Hy is omtrent besig om tussen die golwe te stoei.
Ek sit rustig by die see
met my toebroodjies en rooibostee.

Ek sien 'n man op 'n hoë rots.
Meteens gooi hy sy lyn baie trots
Hy hoop en bid dat die vis gaan byt.
Maar hy moet definitief wag vir 'n onsekere tyd.

Die visserman in 'n ontspannende omgewing.
Skielik is daar aan sy lyn 'n beweging!
Hy gryp sy stok en sy katrol
nou moet hy sy lyn vinnig en sekuur oprol.

Teleurstelling sien jy op sy bruingebrande gesig.
Hy sit 'n swaarder anker op vir meer gewig.
Nog 'n slag probeer
met die hoop die vis byt die keer.

Ek sit rustig by die see.
Dink diep en dit bring heimwee.
Die see gee dieper insig, en
verskaf ook lewenslig

Crash! The sound that changed my life. Part four (by Kurt Abrahams)

I had a nurse coming in every second day to see to my wounds at home. At times I would try and make an excuse for her not to pitch up. I never looked forward to or got excited the days she came. I was in a lot of discomfort when she cleaned and treated my wounds. Although most the stuff she used on my wounds were sponsored, her rates were not low and she only accepted cash as payment. My wife decided to take over from the wound nurse and see to my wounds. Once again, my wife took on another function despite her many duties and responsibilities. As the days went by the challenges continued. Depression once again became my number one enemy. I tried fighting it, but the more I tried the deeper I was slipping into a state of depression once more. I felt helpless. I felt like a total loser. The option to give up was an easy one.

Each new day became more challenging. My family tried their best to uplift me, but to no avail. Although I was on anti-depressants, the depression took over completely. I was suicidal again. I just wanted my life to end. Having my medication close at hand was tempting. I thought of overdosing. This depression held me captive. I felt there was no escape, to the point where I found comfort in my depressed state.

Due to my lack of mobility, and being bedridden, I could not go to see a doctor or a psychologist to receive counselling. I had to fight this battle alone. I prayed. I was not allowing the enemy to get the better of me. I was not going to lose this fight.

Prayer became the most powerful weapon. God helped me to get out of depression. It is amazing how depression can bring one down completely; how it effects the ones close to you. How quickly it makes one lose the zest to live. I thank God for his presence in my life, and how he took me through this tough battle of depression. He gave me back my strength. I focused on Him and His Word. God will never forsake nor leave us. Yesterday, today, tomorrow Jesus is always the same. I was still taking a tablet for anxiety commonly known as a "happy pill" although I'm sure there are much better ways to make one happy. I adopted a positive mindset and started refocusing on the way forward. Things in my home began to stabilise. My wife and my daughters continued to encourage me. They each played a vital role in my life.

Then one day, there was a knock at our front door. It was an official from the finance company regarding my car. My wife brought him to my bedroom where I was laying. I asked him in a sarcastic way what the purpose for his unwelcome visit was. I noticed the arrogance he had on his face. He informed that my car payments were in arrears, and that I had seven days to make the full payment or the bank would have no choice but to repossess my car. He was also very reluctant to hear my side of the story: why I could not afford to pay the installments. I looked up at him with a smile on my face. I told him to check his records and to make sure that he had the correct information. A week earlier my daughter, Candice, offered to pay the balance that was owing on the car. After going through his file, and a phone call to his office, embarrassed he apologised profusely, shaking my hand. I owed nothing on the car. It was fully paid up. He went on to ask what had happened to me; why I was bedridden. I told him. He stood there, speechless. He told me that after so many years of doing this job, my story was the most inspiring story he had heard.

It was on a Friday, midday, when my close friend Brandon Mulder (aka Beefie) popped in for his usual visit. Brandon was the only person who religiously visited me almost every day when I was in hospital, in rehab and at home. I received a call from ABSA Bank informing me that my bond was in arrears and that they were demanding payment. I explained to the official the reason for the arrears. She informed me that the arrangement in place had now expired and that I had to start paying the bond installments in full. Again, I was told that if I'm unable to make the payments, the bank will have no choice but to auction my house. Panic, and anxiety kicked in. My very first thought was what would happen to me and my family. Where are we going to stay? I shared this with Brandon and remember seeing the shocked look on his face. We did not say much more to each other. We just sat there.

Glancing at my phone, I noticed that I had a missed call from my wife. I called my wife on her cell phone and before I could explain to her about the call I received from the bank, she went on to tell me that she received a call from Standard Bank regarding the estate of my late parents. As a beneficiary there was some money due to me from the proceeds of the sale of my parents' house. The money was available to me. When I heard this, I screamed. I burst into tears. I was shaking. I could not believe that this that was happening. Brandon tried to calm me down, not knowing at first what was going on. I gasped for words and with tears washing my face I managed to share the good news. I told him that only the Power of God can do such things. Yes, His promises and great timing is beautiful. I went quiet for a bit and thanked our Heavenly Father for His Grace, Mercies and the Blessings He bestowed on me and others.

It is wonderful when others can see, witness and experience the work of God, even in us. The weekend went by. The first thing Monday morning I notified the bank that I will be paying off, almost my entire bond. An amazing feeling it was, knowing that my family and I will have a roof over our heads.

Ingelegde Kerrievis (deur Samuel Theron)

Ingelegde kerrievis:
'n Tradisionele Goeie Vrydag dis.
Almal geniet dit terdee.
Die servet is geel wanneer ek my hande en mond afvee.

Die beste resepte word gesoek,
want dis geplak in 'n resepteboek.
Mittejalas van toentertyd word gebruik.
Die eindproduk moet mos perfek lyk en ruik.

Dit is ook met liefde ingelê.
Die gaste wat kom kuier wil ook daarvan hê.
Vis in rissies gedoop,
Dis so sterk dat die neuse loop!

Ingelegde kerrievis, deel van Paasfees kultuur.
Bruin suiker en asyn bygevoeg vir soet en suur.
Kerrievis word met hot cross buns geëet.
Wie sal dan dié lekker gereg vergeet?

Die kerrie-reuk hang in die huis.
Bure klop, maar vind niemand tuis.
Vis word in die kerrie sous gelyer.
Hoop nie die familie wil kom kuier.

Die kerrievis is die tyd van die jaar die beste,
maar vis is nou duur in die Kaap se geweste.
Oral waar jy kom kry jy die kerrie reuk hang.
Met my terugblik rol 'n traan oor my wang.

Mitchell's Plain (by Billy Hendricks)

Mitchell's Plain,
Is it only winter in your midst?
Is it only a bloody winter?
When will your season change?
"A generation of drug lords"
"A generation of gangsters"
Will the sun ever shine again?

Will the birds in your court come drink water at my backyard fountain of sweetness?
Will your birds ever have a future?
Mitchell's Plain! Mitchell's Plain!
The Bloody war is killing me
The bloody winter of drugs
The Bloody winter of gangsterism, violence
The Bloody winter of judgment day on all innocent little birds
Mitchell's Plain! Mitchell's Plain!
You are so empty and cold

I wish you have "summer" now
You have such beautiful birds
You have such a beautiful garden
"Don't let the bloody winter destroy it all"
"Set your birds free, yes, set them free"
"Let them fly, let them still try to reach the highest skies"
Mitchell's Plain, Mitchell's Plain I believe one morning when you
Wake up; the summer will be back...

Don't call yourself a man (by Kudakwashe Munemo)

Don't call yourself a man. You are a cold-blooded monster consumed, colonised and conquered by your lust. Stripping in broad daylight, spreading your oversized legs whilst your downsized brain convinces you that the small toddler is your sex mate. You have no shame you rapist. Don't call yourself a man, because you are not.

In their own parents' home...if they knew your mind they would tremble in fear. It's like a lion's den in your evil mind. You harbour ambitions to bed your own little innocent girl – of all the people in the world. You should be her tower of security, but you are not. You are a hyena, preying its own blood. You are a coward! Biological representation of a father: I refuse to call you a man. You are a mutilator, a rapist. Don't call yourself a man.

Daily you stand on the podium preaching righteousness. You call yourself a man of the cloth, but beneath the garment is a wolf in sheep skin. You represent the devil's kingdom. You stand on a pulpit of darkness. I refuse to acknowledge. you as a man of God. You are not a man in shadow of Faith and Trust bestowed onto you. You abuse your female congregants. You even molest tiny girls in Sunday School. You are a rapist!

On paper they call you a man of integrity; a spring of knowledge and a river of wisdom. You are obligated to pass your knowledge onto our children. You are their teacher. I guess I was wrong. Yes, even the school premises a shadow of the Valley of Death. Even there you lurk. You are an evil beast. You are not a man.

Buti Ngomso! (by Dean Ramjoomia)

Buti not today come Ngomso

Ngomso come ngomso go where does ngomso stay

Where is ngomso not today tomorrow Buti Ngomso

Old do I get, sick and weak in my bread wine is my medicine

But ngomso, ngomso never come!

Buti Ngomso

Crash! The sound that changed my life. Part five (by Kurt Abrahams)

It was time for me to arrange my next appointment with my orthopedic surgeon. I required more medical procedures. I always get excited when they confirm the appointments. At times, it takes months before an appointment, but I am always hopeful to hear good news regarding improvement in my mobility. Weeks prior to the appointment, I must arrange both transport and manpower to help carry me to the van. Then, I was unable to sit in a wheelchair. I was placed on a white bed sheet and four guys had to carry me; always mindful not to injure me. In the back of the van was a mattress on which I was placed for my journey to the hospital.

Once at the hospital, I was transferred onto a stretcher and wheeled into trauma where my surgeon examined me from head to toe. I was subjected to and had to endure tremendous pain. The surgeon bent my legs, knees and feet to see if there was any flexibility or movement in my joints. After reviewing my x-rays, he informed that he would perform a procedure called MUA (manipulation under anesthesia): manual therapy treatment to try and improve articular and soft tissue movement while I'm under sedation. Been sent home with this procedure scheduled I had fresh hope that my mobility would improve.

The day of the procedure there was excitement at home. I could not wait to be taken to hospital to undergo the procedure. After almost being in theatre for two hours, I was taken back to the ward to recover. Later that evening as the pain medication began to ware off, I started to experience the most excruciating pain in my joints...the pain was unbearable. The doctor explained that although no surgery was performed, a procedure like this comes with extreme pain as the soft tissue and muscles were exposed to heavy trauma. The slightest movement caused tremendous pain; even pulling the blanket over me caused severe pain.

The following two days the pain continued. I screamed in agony when the nurses turned me to wash me. The morphine administered was not enough. Eventually the dosage was increased. After three days, the pain began to ease, and the swelling started to subside much to my relief.

My joy was short lived. The physiotherapist assigned to me, had to ensure that my muscles and joints remained flexible. She worked my body, which in turn caused more pain. Two weeks later I was sent for x-rays to see whether the procedure worked. Unfortunately, it was not successful. I was once again met with disappointment. The doctor tried to explain the reason for the procedure not working. I debated and was not willing to accept the outcome, but there was nothing I could do, but acknowledge his prognosis. He suggested that I remain in hospital to continue physiotherapy while he and his colleague discuss the next procedure planned for me.

Amidst all the visits I received from my family and friends, I was anxious and nervous about the next procedure. The doctor explained that he was to insert a bolt and screw in my left ankle to straighten out my foot. Although I was happy that he was going to perform another procedure, I still had doubts that the operation would be a success. On the day of my operation, I was once again briefed by the surgeon, before I was wheeled into theatre.

By now I was used to going into theatre. A few hours later I woke up only to find myself again in surgical ICU, 'my home from home' as the nurses called it. As usual I was in pain. My foot was placed in a moon boot to keep it in position. It felt as if I was wearing a boot made of cement. The boot heavy! The nurses still had great difficulty in turning me on my sides to wash me and to change the bedding. They did their best to ensure they made me as comfortable as possible. I am grateful for the kindness and support that nurses gave me and my family. I not only saw the nursing staff in surgical ICU as health practitioners, but as family and my best friends. There was one nurse in ICU, Carmen Robertson, that I became quite attached to. Although she never tolerated my unnecessary moaning and groanings, she would always try and put a smile on my face and make me feel better.

After spending a week in ICU, I was transferred back to the orthopedic ward where I would eventually form the same relationship with the nursing staff. In this section there was one nurse I feared in the beginning, Leah Bam. She was the staff nurse in charge of all the nurses and ensured that the unit ran efficiency. She tolerated no nonsense from the nurses or patients. I appreciated Bam. We became good friends.

It's almost a decade later. I relive the sounds of yesterday. I am thankful when I hear the voice of my grandchild. I am loved. I can see and touch and hear. I write stories of my experience and God's Grace on my life. I write about the funnies and the not so funnies. I was given a second chance. I write about the Sound of Jesus in my heart.

We Love Them (by Jurgen Namupira)

Raise your heart oh dear poet!
let your inner voice speak on behalf of your eyes
together we can change the world,
never for the worst;
our intentions are kind...
kind to love them,
them that have been victimised,
victimised and given names,
names that kill their confidence.

Rise oh dear poet!
drag your pen to your paper
and let your ink make as much noise as possible.
STOP IT! ENOUGH IS ENOUGH!
let's see your pen declare
PEACE! And share your life experience.

write, write and write dear writer,
write until the ink turns into a song,
a song loud enough for this world to hear
the sounds of your soul.

Roar like a lion my fellow poets and writers,
let your port of exit for words be ready

and your voices audible to all nations,
we are ready to make all nations kind,
kind to love,
love them…
for the violation and evil and mayhem
is our sin…
indirectly directly,
but the fact remains
we still do, and still share that sound.

***

My travel through southern Africa was probably the most daring thing I had ever done. It pushed all my boundaries. I was out of character or coming into character. I was once unafraid to share my love for God. I had confidence anew to speak what my words had always been about, since my earliest understanding. I write about God and my silly thoughts of God. I write about my Father in Heaven. I write about Jesus, my friend who has never changed even in those days and times when I was not a good friend.

I remember returning home. I was 28. I thought I was rid of my sins. Two months after I returned from my journey through Southern Africa, I wrecked my dad's car. I drove off from the scene of the accident. It was past 2am on a

Saturday morning. On the corner of Voortrekker Road, in Goodwood, a group of guys appeared on the accident scene. I was drunk. I think my last stop was Open Arms. I crashed into a woman's car at a traffic intersection. I convinced myself that she was in the same state as I; drunk. Yet, my drunk had caused the accident. I still don't know if those guys at the accident scene were real. Yet, they chanted: 'Go broe. Go! If they catch you, you will be in shit.' After making sure that the lady in the other car was fine, I drove off. Yet, I neglected to see her shock, which I felt. I had lodged this experience so far in my mind, I had forgotten what it was like spending the night – privileged – in a cell of my own, whilst the others were squealing 'Why does he get all the regard?'

Some strings were pulled and the same day I was out. Not free, I still had to go to court to plea.

I remember the doctor taking my blood, asking why I was doing this to me. Handcuffed, shoved...I guess all was necessary. Fired my lawyer and stood up alone in court. I knew God was with me. I had come home, to Him.

Returning to the sounds of home (by Taryn Haynes-Smart)

The pre-recorded voice calmly announces that our descent into Cape Town has begun. This is followed a few minutes later by the pilot's instruction to the crew to take their seats for landing. The lights dim inside the cabin in preparation. It is Autumn in Cape Town and nightfall comes early. Outside my window, I see the lights of home twinkling across the Cape Town landscape. Soon, I will hear the sounds from home.

As I pull up to the house, I hear my dogs barking enthusiastically welcoming my return. A little brown snout pushes through the drawn curtains, and peaks through the lounge window, before dashing to the door, as if she was the lookout confirming that it really is me. It doesn't really matter how long I am away – my canine greeting is much the same for ten minutes or ten days. I smile in anticipation of the clamour awaiting me. The garage door closes behind me, shutting out the sounds outside.

I barely enter the house. My inquisitive pups encircle me eagerly making it difficult for me to get through the doorway. The bedtime routine is underway. I hear the kettle boiling. I hear the sweet melodic sound of my daughter's voice as she prepares for bed. Awaiting her cup of tea and my imminent arrival, she entertains her audience (her dad and a rather large assortment of plush toys and dolls) with a story from the day. The chatter pauses as the dogs' announcement of my homecoming reaches her.

I hear the bedroom door knock against the cupboard as it succumbs to the rush of air created in her haste to greet me. I hear her dad's cautionary appeal to be careful trailing behind her as she speeds around the corner. I have just enough time to drop my bags and brace myself as she throws her arms around me. I am whisked through to the bedroom and ushered to the chair, like a queen being shown to her throne. Dad is now free to resume the tea making. While he revels in a few minutes of quiet, I am regaled with what feels like a hundred colourful stories delivered all at once. Then it's my turn to read a bedtime story. She chimes in – filling in the gaps and questioning for clarity. The story read, teeth brushed, and devotion shared, I tuck her into bed. My face shares the smile in my heart as she gives thanks, along with her dad, for all we have.

Lights out. In mock sternness, I remind her, for a third time, that it's time for bed. Softly she responds with words that melt my heart every time: "I love you mommy. I missed you. Welcome home!"

Yes, once again, I find myself thanking the sounds from home, my home.

Our home (by Gavin Joachims)

Dear Lord, I thank you for Your Love for us. I thank you Father for the peace we find in Your Presence. Hallowed be Your Name throughout the ages. Beautiful are You, my Father; my Creator. I love You Lord. I love You.

***

I guess my life had always been - and will be - honouring my mom and my dad. They truly understand me, better than most. They have shown me love. In all I have done and do, they supported me; even from the beyond, and even in-spite of me.

I thank my father and mother. I thank our fathers and our mothers. I ask forgiveness when we, have wronged them.

I ask our Mother City to forgive us all, for the sins we have brought to her shores. I ask in Jesus Name, that she continues to nurture us. I ask in Jesus Name that she continues to fill us with creativity, love and peace that raises from her deep. Beautiful sounds coming from the hearts of those, here read.

Cape Sounds.

Authors

Abednigo Mlesh Nyuka
Ané Williams
Billy Hendricks
Dean Ramjoomia
Donovan Beukes
Gaireyah Fredericks
Gavin Joachims
Jonathan van Beulen
Jurgen Namupira
Kurt Abrahams
Marius Williams
Mrs. Bosman-Adams
Samuel Theron
Taryn Haynes-Smart

Gavin Joachims Publishing’
Email: gavinjoachimspublishing@gmail.com

www.ingramcontent.com/pod-product-compliance
Lightning Source LLC
Chambersburg PA
CBHW032254070726
47590CB00016B/2792

* 9 7 8 0 6 2 0 8 4 3 1 2 6 *